WE
SHED
OUR
SKIN
LIKE
DYNAMITE

FIRST POETS SERIES 20

Guernica Editions Inc. acknowledges the support of
the Canada Council for the Arts and the Ontario Arts Council.
The Ontario Arts Council is an agency of the Government of Ontario.
We acknowledge the financial support of the Government of Canada.

CONYER CLAYTON

WE
SHED
OUR
SKIN
LIKE
DYNAMITE

GUERNICA
EDITIONS

TORONTO · BUFFALO · LANCASTER (U.K.)
2020

Michael Mirolla, general editor
Elana Wolff, editor
Cover and interior design: Rafael Chimicatti
Cover image: Graphic Compressor/Shutterstock
Guernica Editions Inc.
287 Templemead Drive, Hamilton (ON), Canada L8W 2W4
2250 Military Road, Tonawanda, N.Y. 14150-6000 U.S.A.
www.guernicaeditions.com

Distributors:
Independent Publishers Group (IPG)
600 North Pulaski Road, Chicago IL 60624
University of Toronto Press Distribution,
5201 Dufferin Street, Toronto (ON), Canada M3H 5T8
Gazelle Book Services, White Cross Mills
High Town, Lancaster LA1 4XS U.K.

First edition.
Printed in Canada.

Legal Deposit – First Quarter
Library of Congress Catalog Card Number: 2019946878
Library and Archives Canada Cataloguing in Publication
Title: We shed our skin like dynamite / Conyer Clayton.
Names: Clayton, Conyer, author.
Series: First poets series (Toronto, Ont.) ; 20.
Description: Series statement: First poets series ; 20 | Poems.
Identifiers: Canadiana 20190158433 |
ISBN 9781771835091 (softcover)
Classification: LCC PS8605.L395 W4 2020 | DDC C811/.6—dc23

for my sisters, Page and Cat

Contents

III ──────────────────────────────

"All people live
how they want

over and over
levelled by time"

— **I** —

"Our thoughts bound in the open air."

Seeds

I pray to catch on fire,
to get caught up
in a mercifully
lightening storm,

burn my body back
to earth. The woods

are overcrowded. Stillness
lost, boardrooms and clearings.
We competed for the sun,

reaching out for the last
solar flare, arcing slowly
over you lying still on the couch.
Mortgage research and persistent fungi.
Abortions whispered
into rotting logs and deer hooves.
I nearly slipped hard
in the rain water,
the thick coating of mustard.
Just missed
disturbing a mosquito
nest brimming

with potential babies.
What kind of father would you have been?

Blackout

Maybe if we hang
enough butterflies on invisible strings
we'll enjoy it here, be fooled

into a smile by bright colours
and a song on repeat.

Lullabies cramp your style —
your legs drawn
into a ball. See you tonight

maybe? The music builds
forced, sheets pulled tight
over crumbs.

The sun's been shining
while you've been sleeping, shining for hours
through a blind broken window.

Full Sunlight

Two men came and brought down the ivy
mammoth with whirling blades, cables
slung over the topmost branches
like some military operation
taking down the enemy —
　　　　only a wizened tree
　　　　two hundred years old
　　　　dry rotting from the inside out
　　　　strangled by living vines.

Wood chips fill the air
as the family next door sits
on their porch at mother's wake.

She died last night in her sleep, obese and unexpected.
And the man we suspect of having a meth lab
is crying in the street. Crying with sawdust on his face.
As they struggle to remove her
from the house, dismembered branches hit
the ground and tear the earth apart.

I stand engulfed by a hollow stump,
full sunlight streaming through my windows.

Mud Relish

These nights are white, moulding
minds empty as the air is full.

We're desperate for what's buried,
head in a pile of rocks.

What colour is the sun?
Still yellow you suppose.

A gas pipeline
marked on wet concrete.

Mud is slicker than ice these days.
There's no dry ground to wipe your boots on.

Recoil

I've gotten used to continual stings,
his hand on her

cut pants, thorny iris
hidden, jaws clamped shut
on a horse bit, chomp
and chaw — leave
tobacco stained teeth and fingertips
for a cleaner glass.
I am the one packing books
in wet cardboard.

I would happily tear my skin
on foreign stones, crush my femurs
on a farm — a pasture
with a rusted tractor.

Will you toil

under the summer sun?
Pick berries with a steel thrush
and live for free?
We'll all be under a new tragic sky;

attempting to find comedy
in a sunset, a finch's snapped neck
and feathers, a woodchuck's
paring of bucks and bones.
All in the angle of our eyes.
Tow, tread, sow.

Dock Drunk

There is nothing subtle in a cinder block
cabin, animal curtains; bear, snake, and lace.

In your footsteps, ruins of rocks, the frantic mess
we made, everyone stretching in their sleep.

Someone forgot to shut the door, but only rain
and music slip in. Yeah, I think I heard something slip

when I was alone last night, a turtle in the water,
lonely
in cricket company, the birds oblivious and silent.

Intake

The wind bursts
around the corner
of the house,
catches breath
before saying —

Unpopular Knowledge

The trees edge
        and groan. Live
slowly between our unruly days,
speak in a cricket's rub
        and frog song.

Winter is one
        short night. Short
for the time they wake and bud,
bloom and shed,
        resting in ice inches deep.

A lifetime spent in yearning.

Skin Shield

We have to wait for the wind
to calm. I stand

facing the road, the field
behind — hazy with black butterflies.

Let's rest at the joining, the place
between two leaves.

I almost lost you in your skin,
pulsing on a fallen tree trunk.

Broken Leaf

I float within thin walls of membrane,
surrounded by shadows, sunlight
shining through translucent skin.
Distinguish plant from leg, spindle
from soft, tiptoe from whisper. I've changed

colour, plucked from rest
to be crushed and shredded
between foreign skinned fingers,
ripped at my cytoplasmic seams.
All my intricacy reduced to stains
on pants and palms.

Splinters grow whole and whole again.

Drop me into brick and steel and granite,

where my home grows wider
under weight of footsteps.

Tending Towards the Fall

It's easy to be led into a cave's open
mouth, tongue lagging. To sit straight
backed against a slow drip. *It seems obvious*

the colours are brighter on your back,
she said, flicking bees from her sweat.

Flies tread over titles
like a path towards peace; gods
in every season except winter.
She would let them
eat her skin away, gladly

accept a brand new breeze, winds
hushed by the rocks' sediment, a sentiment
we've all failed to label, and yet

the only property that matters: our thoughts

bound in the open air.

Bone Bed

She finds comfort in a collarbone,
angles fit for smaller jaws.
Draws a drop of warmth

like sap from axe wounds,
fast-paced in a pine
tree, shoulders ribboned
to the trunk, half off
the thinly padded floor.

She set it out for you, neatly,
mirrors and chalked nostrils
flaring. It's the very shawl
she wears to cover
a thin white dress, stitched
with longing. I find
crystals to this day,
but only on my hands,

instead of in a star
or a galaxy too big to slip
a ring over, during a waltz out
of time, too well rehearsed.

There are nights when
we shut the curtains
to deter the sunrise, pile on blankets
like pie crust. We're melted in the middle,
elbows crispy, cooking
in collectivity, marinating madness.

Home

My feet blackened like catfish
on the flat tar roof. Sitting
over my own bedroom, dirty
toes dangling, eyes
on the road past the mailbox,
past the red breasted robins
hearing insects make their way
through the soil. Wait, wait
and plunge
into the earth.
Same earth of my body.
Same earth of her body.
Same earth of her ashes
poured
into lakewater.
Same earth
on my feet.
Her body
in a bird's belly. Her body
dropped on a windshield. Her body
scrubbed off at a gas station. Her body
poured onto the sidewalk with the soapy water.
Her body sinking
into the concrete's cracks. Her body
sinking. Her body
sinking
her body joining her body
rising
into the air her body
dispersing my memories dispersing her body

my mind thinning out and joining
and disappearing and finding her body again
inside me. Sitting ten years old
on a flat tar roof, waiting
to see her car pulling into the driveway,
to see her get out and smile and take me
home, take me home, take me home,
please mommy, take me home.

Trace

We leave our skin on rock
faces, dance vertically
on cliffs, let our sweat
drop for miles.

I'm back, alone.
I existed once
in this place,
like every place.

Amber

It is in this place with no skin
cells on the shelves, where the ringing
of porcelain brings excess
that's only enough when it stains
the saucer amber.

Where leaves sustain a man,
keep his sunken folds seated, his soles
from oil slicks and the rub of flesh
on rope — pressure only more brandy can heal.

The texture of the air has changed,
entering his ear for no reason at all.

He draws pesos from a leather pouch.

After Green Is Gold

A man mouth-
pixeled speech to me,
humming
to nudge the notes off
                    the ledge
of his lips. Buzzing
wood and spittle, spiders
sauntering over strings
pound out waves like words.

Wild heather strikes
the same chord.

His roots twist up
into hips and down
through hardened
beetle graves. Bark peels
like dead skin, cracks
in callused fingertips.
An orchid breaks through
caverns of pulsating brass

and all the unlit corners
of all the unlit rooms.

Shower

The show is set to start
so I slip lazily out.

I just want to walk, to keep
my eyes from good folk like you;

a lifeboat drifting
in the wrong direction.

Focus on:
       the termite bled wood
       stone chiselled cheekbones
       stolen sand
       grasping hands
       the leap over granite
       a stiff step forward on a locked knee
       disconnected hands below my bra

Somehow, the suds hold together.
Hopping from teacup to saucer
and onto a dirty curb, crawling
as ants crawl, legs unseen,
thin
as moss between shoe
bottoms and rocks.

I stick to your fingertips,
solid as breath.

— II —

"Who will maintain this mess of skin?"

Trap

We came home
late, caught

a spider in a cocktail glass
and watched him;

free, fearless
among giants, silent
on a stranger's walls.

Southern Belle

Saunter daintily across hot brown coals,
spin parasols around dizzied
heads, beckon you to my bed.
Please, please, oh please just
stay inside awhile — you must think
me old — too close. Typical
ideas you tend to hold against tile
ceilings, questioning a stain. No
it's the method itself that makes you wonder,
envision a stamped hand against your cheek,
my arms wrapped in transparent tape, packed gently,
just so long as I can fit. *This is your real*

home. You've never been
your own person.
We're bound
by our lives, but we can tip
the glass to the left and avoid
the foam. Dip a finger in forehead
oil, make it bubble away, ready
to drink
and be drunk, despite the knocking.
Are you even in there?

Neighbours

I sit knock knocking back beers
with a slurred and blurring woman
on her seat's edge tonguing
at the bartender, pulling her
scarf below the collar, colouring her
world amber-toned and stained, drained
to the last lick of what could possibly
have slipped in her centre, grinding
a year's worth of vomit and spinning ceilings

with her boot heels, dancing for a lottery
ticket, a free pass, telling everyone how good they smell.

I guess it's the older crowd tonight.
I'll be there in ten, I type. My stomach rising.

The last sip is always the worst.

Burning

Some nights you don't end up here.
A dark beer steals
your padded paws to cooler cushions.

I know it's hot, so I borrowed
my friend's fan, a blade
for our bedside, but it's really only mine.

Distracted Backs

I think your fire alarm battery is about to die, you say
as you pull back your hair to keep it from my face.
Does it always feel
this good? you ask,
cartoon pupils and heavy brow
questioning. No, I lie.

We dance with other couples, exchange
loaded glances over freckled shoulders
and distracted backs.
I'd tell you a dream I had if I hadn't forgotten.

The fire alarm's still beeping,
warning, warning, and we're warming
one another in loosened grips.

Setting an Alarm

In a Bathrobe

Sweet potato sitting soggy
in a doggy bag next to you
and a leftover oyster roll.
You tracked in snow
from spite,
despite my
pushing away. No.
I said, no. I'm busy.
You're relentless, you know?

Untied

And then you brought a cream
and pesto pizza in your workplace
box from across slickened
streets, so thoughtfully.

Moments after I pushed him

out, I begged you to stay.

In Bed

I sleep alone on purpose,
with regret.

Lid

You've got some sun, he said,
like a poem, he said.
Silhouetted in shades of moonlight.

It's never really been a problem, no,
never really been an issue at all,
until you raised it —

a toast, a waltz, a tip
of your melted wax hat
in my direction.

United Air

We drink beer from pale blue cans
on the front porch, and talk about those last seven years.
I'm sorry, just so sorry. We're always sorry.

We take another drink.

I returned that guy's broth pot and colander. Left them
outside his shitty apartment door with a note
written on the back of an online airplane reservation.

This Is the Bandage

I can feel the rising edges, peeled
away by a pulsing tide, salt; my skin
wicks up moisture greedily.
The cover falls free.

The feel of this spiral is different; greased
and peppered, kept small. We fiddle
away the moments, sit inches
back in our own skulls, maintain distance
from our eyes. That soft patch
is already exposed. An open wound —

vulnerable.

I scrub the pans
from any sign of use,
wishing life was like this.

Buildup

A bruised unpolished nail
begging to be let go,
demanding a rip of the cuticle,
of the surrounding skin smashed
on pavement the night before last,
caught between vodka
tonic and dizzy whiz truly
fried potatoes, greasy pool
sticks and an undiscerning lens —

Catching what I don't want
known, recording the fall
flat on my back
in the parking lot, legs
tangled in chains
and flimsy rubber reflectors —

Explaining bruises to in-laws,
jams to children, lacerations
to aunts and uncles, feeling
their stares as I pick and fester,
press my print against a tabletop
just hoping the pressure will stop —

We Hit the Mattress

past midnight,
knees meddling
movement.

A world is
spinning
under your skin.

Swallow the Seeds

We hide rebels under wood, and beware
of tales, watermelon trees
rooted in bile.
Who can tell if we're crying or praying?
We turn our faces into the sun. There's nothing
left to look at, so I recreate an imprint in the mud,
clear crumbs from my bed sheets,
never buy crackers again.

It's ineffective.
The glare makes it obvious.
Fold your hands.
Swallow the seeds.

Feel death,
but in this way: poured
over firmly potted orchids.

Bug-Eyed

A flattering newcomer lands
modestly in my eye.

Gentle spindles,
rub flowers into me.

Your shell expands:
my world, your inside halls.

I close my lids
over your six gone-legs, gripping
a tickle to my nervous signals —

optical tap and buzz. I pour
lilies on my breakfast grains,
all stares and blinking.

I Can Finally See You

from boy to metal
mermaid, south-end cigarette,
        cough in painted smocks. No,
            not purple, my mother is a lawyer,

chained standing proud in centre courtyard, tackled
    from a concrete stool.

Why haven't we spoken in all this time?

It's really a tear at this point,
blisters only go

        so deep, walking with your belly out,
        tanned stubble from orange sweat,
wet at a festival, sharing stalls and frozen pretzels,
        granola stuck in my pocket.

But it's more than just that.

We've changed. Picked a tune and trashed it.
I've showered, salted, snipped, and fallen.
        Dropped in buckets and bedpans,
            tangled in sands,

for once not pretending.

Convinced

This is what was fine, this is what was fine, this is what was

— a faucet turned on
pouring itself out.
Cotton to soak the drip, because yes we're all fine here —

move along
across the sea. Board
a plane with a set of cards,
a handcrafted game of islands.
I make trouble

in the next room so you can show me how it feels
to touch a hand again,
all the photographs deleted.
It's hard to pass up and I never have
before, but suddenly my stomach
rejects what's been roasting
for some time now; a raindrop
on an air-conditioner to keep me

awake, to plug my ears with just how fine
I am, how great great great I am,
not concerned, no not
at all, not
me, not me.

A Month and a Year

Your finger tracing my forehead,
What are those eyes for? All back
in your head and looking
like death, a rehearsal

in a parking lot, scolded for being
in a tree with a drink —

the only place I can see or feel clearly
anymore, since you had to choose

this month to apologize, to drop
a faint and distant line then
disappear again —
into a fog of blonde hair and swollen skin.

I don't want this.

I'd been breathing clearly for months.
So I refuse, but refusal does nothing
but repeat and convince, repeat
and convince no one

that I've dropped off clear, that I wade
in the heavy air alone, suck
noodles from a bowl. Cucumber and curry
slip through the chopsticks, lost

at the bottom. A fish living on sun.

Etiquette

This is no longer appropriate dinner conversation.
                                    (your ghost
                                    in the grains)
Elbows off the table.
Hold your knife in your good hand.
Slow down and close your damn mouth.
Posture is important, your bones stacked neatly
inside. Don't let the fluids mix. Don't let her touch
the crust. Be impenetrable as your father.
As his unsmiling
portrait at the bottom of the basement stairs.
As his grim
thin mouth. Speak

only of proper things. Don't speak
of spirits. Don't speak

of her body. Thick
carpet indenting her skin,
a lighter loosely in hand.
Dinner isn't the time for unscientific beliefs,
vegetables roaming across a plate
unchecked. Her body ripening
in the gap days. The bloated
hours. Air moving clearly
in her throat. Throat cleared.
Palms on the table.
What did I say?

Family History

Blades shudder against concrete, seeking something
soft to butcher.
We long to make a lasting mark.
Trimmed hedges and gently shaped sand.
A legacy of ice-filled cups and swollen stomachs;
the pages of your family
written cold
and yellowing in a cellar.
Who will maintain this mess of skin?
Who will shape the glass blades of your past? An old man
squats on the sidewalk and tends his shrinking
plot with garden shears.
Can we work with the weeds?
Can we stop fighting natural symmetry, the grooves
carved by wind and winter?
Sinking proof
the sun rose again.
The rising evidence it set.
Pick me, pluck me, rake me. Arrange me in a vase with water.
Bring me inside, ensure my demise.
What a beautiful centrepiece I make. What a rotting
heap of once living sinew. Keep me connected.
Dirt to core to dirt again. The roots
stretch further in stillness.

What You Actually Lost

I convince myself
     death comes from the wind

I kill you
     with my exhale
     with the roughly chopped garlic

I dream of my mother
     a baby gets measles

I put on the wrong album
     you wreck your car

I see a darkness in my own eyes
     a tumour starts to form

I focus on the bruised skin of an orange to protect myself
This isn't unfamiliar

I've run cemetery paths casually
and been scolded by a woman
sitting at her dead husband's grave
I've stared at the turning leaves — overlooked
the names; noticed the wildflowers, not
the freshly-turned earth they sprouted from

I woke today
     with the image of blood spilling
from an umbilical cord onto my frantic palms

      diving naked into a snowbank
screaming the news of death at strangers

My dreams seep
into lightness —
into daytime thoughts

I woke heavy

as my mother's calm voice,
a dark brown stain on the carpet.

— III —

"How efficiently we grieve ..."

Instructional

How to Touch a Hand

Be slow, and wait
for the back room to empty.
Lose your lost love's name,

the one that leaves your throat raw.
Don't you know
she dances like that for everyone?

Accept the Erasure

The best we can do is lose.
Embrace the fins
cutting the sea floor.

It's only a darkness;
a returned envelope,
our meat cut thin.

Solder

       your edges and shorting wires.
Avoid excess.
You're overheated, and liable
for the burns

you create. I wanted
to come here,
consider your potential.
I realize how this comes across.

You May Not Reach 65

Your nicest sweater — cashmere
bought in an open market, teeth flashing,
slapped fish and pomegranates

in a straw basket, a preordained jar of spices.
Tap, tap, crush and pour,
finally it's you. Only you.

I avert my gaze, dried
spinach and lamb,
your unwashed hair, your surprise age.

How can you be proud?
Your eyes are lost and wrinkled in the light.

Too much? you ask me. *Too much?*
A struggle
to grasp. Don't
forget which mug is yours.

Sleep Breathes

I woke you double
handed, cupped in a pillow
for unfiltered release. The dreams

I had last night sniff and roar
like broken plumbing,

the uneven footfall of the mind.
You can't run

far from a week of heavy drinking,
stumbling home hand in hand, secrets
spoken in darkness.

I'm practicing how I'll lie in my coffin.

Goodwill Mug

I sink into your absence.
You said too much. Yawning
buildings and steel, all to forget
and bury myself in paper.

To lay me down.
Lay me down and forget.

Like your lost sheaths,
like *backwoods whores,*
like yesterday's roasted red potatoes
stuck to aluminum foil. Soggy
fish floats in peppered milk.

Throw it all away, all the silk, all
the gartered clinks and strokes.
Pull the strings from your stomach
and let them
scrape
through your fidgeting fingers.

Lay me down.
Lay me down and forget.

Suddenly Empty Spaces

Wind camps
in a wet nose.
Alcoholic sweat.
A dripping serenade
floats in foam, cold
on cold on cold.

*

We were born herb
and booze laden, spent
breast feeding stealing a cup
here and there, pissing
for warmth down scaled legs
and rolling.

*

Sea-salted stems, caramelized lady
bugs. The smell of your shattered wingtips.

A message in your pores
flows through suddenly
empty spaces.

*

We were born liced,
frizzed and grizzled, picked

from desk bottoms into plaque mouths,
the dried spit of adolescence.

*

The season's first loss
of green
escapes like resin
from a woodpecker's home.
Lapped up in an eager kiss.
Always cold
on cold on cold.

A Record on Repeat

We sent ourselves through
the air, a kiss to the stars
planted on your best friend's cheek, a record
on repeat to reference how I feel,
to reassure what I already know; that
an adjustment is necessary.

I am repulsed to notice myself.
An empty arm-nest, longing.

This foils our plans for independence,
for nights spent in confidence.

I'm just an inconsolable fold
of skin over nerves.

I'm just the person I need to be,
all the things I can't stand to hear you say.

I Deal With It

I amp myself, lightning bolts and lawn mower cords,
sit me on my ass.

Blow myself, tongue and stickers, right
out of the pond.

Swim in it. Scare away the birds
and small children.

Sand in hummus, sand in underwear.
Eat it anyway.

I own this body,

        sometimes.

I fuck to own
the fucking.

My body means
nothing by default.

It has meaning
when I decide it does.

The Screen Comes Off Easily

You text me to say
you crawled out the window
to the balcony
of your hotel room
on the 26th floor,
wind around the sides
of buildings tearing
your hair out, tearing you off
like the beetle you released
to starlight and concrete.

How efficiently we grieve

depends not on the body itself,
the colour coding,
the spice drawers.
Put it back
where you found it.
Put it back quickly
before I notice the gap,
the continuing nights spent alone,
the ones I asked for,

the steps heavy and shuffling regardless.

          *

She left the long list of her leaving out plain:
          her body
          cigarette burned

blanket
long list
groups of letters
tattered sweaters
turquoise nightgown
moles sun-spotted (palm backs and cheeks)

The tapestry behind her weighted down with
the smallest flower repeated,
the smallest flower, small and blooming widely.

*

We sit with our food
groups grouped
in thick bricks of colour
on our plates.
No need
to supplement this existence
with the slow release
of how much we know
once our toes are off the edge.

How little we know.

And the lightness with which
you come back inside.

The Sky Has to Cool at Some Point

It's the month of metal and cornstalks, lilting
tunes written with a glacier

in mind, groaning slowly
over the earth's plates, a music

heard fathoms deep in our bones,
but more so in a leaf
shrunk into
itself,

a life spent
in drought and wind.

Reach into the Hollows

When I was a child I plunged
my arm into the exposed
roots of creek-bed trees.
I shoved my small

hand deep, knowing
the scales that slinked beyond
my reach, that embedded
themselves deeper
            into their leavings.

There's a rhythm
to it. An ice-age old
cycle. A fishing line caught
in the bedrock. Our gills still
functioning freely.

We find it in
our leavings when

we shed our skin
like dynamite. Smote
and sparkling. Relishing
in the drift of smoke upwards.

        In our leaving

the birds stretch
our skin beyond

recognition, our teeth
dropping like leaves

on a moving river.
We've grown
into large bushes and someone
must hedge this. Cut us
into dolphins and teacups and shapes

resembling humans
once living.

In our leaving they'll dress us in our old worn clothes.
In our leaving we grow taller.
In our leaving we thicken and thin,
reach into the hollows
of an old oak and come out
empty and arid and dry.

We walk circles in a public garden,
incorporate the sound
of engines into birdsongs.
A song is a hum is a song —
like humming, thrums
        of our leaving

the way we calmly   left
the womb, moistly   left

on the ground
to wait for the rain,
to rinse the mothers
from our flesh.

Over from the Start

Crickets bellow that time turns
over, and you
bat rocks with sticks
on a windless day. You'll be sore
from twisting, filthy from finding

a pattern, serpents
etched on fossils, a fist
into drywall, a swing
and a sparkle,
missed
three times and you're done.

Recurrent

If the river stood still it would
        become a mountain.

Built on the backs of mallards
        and trout. Their bodies etched
in stone; we dig them out

        and blow the dust off. Rebuild
their existence in code, digital preening,
virtually nesting in the shade by the bushes,
gliding on invisible currents we transmit
to one another every moment of our lives.
We cut it back for aesthetics, but
it will always grow. We always come back

despite the butchering. Flowers
        mimic bugs mimic
branches mimic branches mimic
        bugs. Design isn't so different,

my skin spotting in the sun, so I can sink
into the sand and wooded places. The edges
we use most often harden and yellow.

        We too can run on stone.
We too migrate over oceans.
Go south for winter. Hunker
        down and hibernate.

We too call out desperately
for mates, pray our voices rise

over the din of engines and radios
and seeds spiralling through the air.
We hold tight to the backs of butterflies
to be carried somewhere fertile
and stable, where our needs will be fulfilled.
           We welcome the dark

thriving worms. Leave them
           under our nails. The sheen
of river feathers. A crackling exoskeleton.
           The lichen children scrape and drop.
The ground it all comes back to.

We cannot escape the rushing water.
Scales skilfully sweep
the surface, break the tension,
a wooden spoon laid over a boiling pot.
We touch the surface.
Press our palms down to release

the excess, count backwards
from ten, nine, eight, seven, six, five —
           stop halfway because
we know the ending. It dumps out somewhere.
An aqueduct or colander. Headlong

waterfall. Sharp turn. Sharp breath. Collect
hair from the drainpipe. The inevitable
footpath-tread next to concrete.

Our bones crave softness.
       We are worn down
layer by layer, no need to relay this
       message. We will hear it

       no matter what. The subtle
       budding despite months of ice.

       We want to be wind-
weathered, but soft to touch; a mountain
       pulled apart by shifting plates, slowly
becoming a river again.

How We Burn

We may resemble embers

      draped on the dock, the horizon slimy.

A ladder of snake-skins. The dark difference.

      We're so much calmer, a glowing revolution.

I almost didn't answer you.

Sediments

We come from the tall
grass, knotted trees.

The space between
earth and sky.

I asked the clouds for a message
and received an answer crumbled
in a lifetime of rocks.

Keep quiet in case you miss it.

Acknowledgements

Thanks to the editors and judges of the following publications and contests in which these poems first appeared, some in different versions and under different titles:

ARC: "Seeds," 2017 Diana Brebner Winner

Bywords: "Family History"; "How We Burn"

Chaudiere Books Blog: "Skin Shield"

Coven Editions: "The Sky Has to Cool at Some Point"; "Unpopular Knowledge"

experiment-o: "I Deal With It," "Southern Belle," "Lid," "Intake," and "Instructional"

The Fiddlehead: "Recurrent," Honourable Mention, *The Fiddlehead*, 2018 Annual Poetry Contest

Goodwill Zine, #7: "Is This Too Much?"

Mochila Review: "Full Sunlight"; "Recoil"

PACE: "Tending Towards the Fall"

Prairie Fire: "Home"; "What You Actually Lost," Third Place, 2017 *Prairie Fire* Poetry Contest

Talking About Strawberries: "Setting an Alarm"

The Café Review: "Over From the Start"

The Harbour Review: "Seeds" reprinted in a special abortion--themed issue.

The League of Canadian Poets, Poetry Pause: "What You Actually Lost"

The Snail Mail Review: "Bone Bed"

The Tau Creative Journal: "Trap"

U of L White Squirrel: "Broken Leaf"

Audio/musical versions of "Recurrent" and "Home" appeared on my 2018 collaborative album with Nathanael Larochette, *If the river stood still*. Thank you to everyone who supported that project.

Thank you to the many friends, family, and writing peers who read versions of these poems and helped me see this manuscript through in many different capacities especially Dan Mollema, Justin Martin, Page Packer, and Cat Gallagher.

A huge thank you to Martha Greenwald for your keen attention, editing, and consistent support. Your edits on the order of the original version of this manuscript were immensely helpful. Some of these poems were written over a decade ago in my first university poetry course, which you taught. Your input meant a lot to me then, and it means a lot to me still.

Forever gratitude and love to Nathanael Larochette for your edits, presence and constancy. For being the master of titles. You helped me cultivate the calm to see this manuscript, among many things, more clearly.

Big shout out to all my fellow members of & Co Collective, and all of my poetry family and friends in Ottawa. There are too many of you to name! The support and friendship of the Ottawa community is hugely inspiring to me. I am honoured to workshop, read, and share space with all of you.

Thanks so much to my editor Elana Wolff at Guernica Editions for understanding this collection better than me sometimes, and seeing something in it worth publishing. Working with you has been such a pleasure. I couldn't ask for a better experience from my debut full-length. Thanks so much for making it so.

To the designer of my cover, Rafael Chimicatti, such gratitude! Working with you has been so easy and you brought the vague vision I had into focus better than I could have hoped.

Thanks to everyone at Guernica Editions: publishers Michael Mirolla and Connie McParland, and associate publisher and publicist Anna van Valkenburg.

And to you, reader—thank you for taking the time and energy to delve into my little poetic universe.

About the Author

Conyer Clayton was born and raised in Louisville, Kentucky, and now happily calls Ottawa home. She has six chapbooks: *Trust Only the Beasts in the Water* (above/ground press), /(post ghost press) *Undergrowth* (bird, buried press), *Mitosis* (In/Words Magazine and Press), *For the Birds. For the Humans.* (battleaxe press), and *The Marshes* (& Co Collective, 2017). She released a collaborative album with Nathanael Larochette, *If the river stood still,* in August 2018. Her work appears in *ARC, Prairie Fire, The Fiddlehead, The Maynard, Puddles of Sky Press,* and other publications. She won *ARC's* 2017 Diana Brebner Prize, placed third in *Prairie Fire's* 2017 Poetry Contest, and received honourable mention in *The Fiddlehead's* 2018 poetry prize. She is a member of the sound poetry ensemble Quatuor Gualuor, and writes reviews for *Canthius. We Shed Our Skin Like Dynamite* is her first full-length collection of poems.

Printed in January 2020
by Gauvin Press,
Gatineau, Québec